LIFE'S JOURNEY

LIFE'S JOURNEY
(VOLUME 1)

JON F. GLEMAN

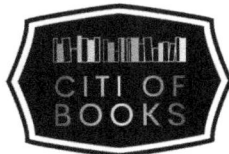

CITI OF
BOOKS

CITIOFBOOKS, INC.
3736 Eubank NE Suite A1
Albuquerque, NM 87111-3579
www.citiofbooks.com
Hotline: 1 (877) 389-2759
Fax: 1 (505) 930-7244

Ordering Information:

Quantity sales. Special discounts are available on quantity purchases by corporations, associations, and others. For details, contact the publisher at the address above.

Printed in the United States of America.

ISBN-13:	Softcover	978-1-960952-08-0
	eBook	978-1-960952-09-7
	Hardcover	978-1-960952-09-7

Library of Congress Control Number: 2023907601

Gleman's memoir shares the joys of a child coming of age in Miami in the 1950s and 60s who had a deep love of the natural world. A biologist and ecologist, the author ran and operated a small mail-order bookshop on the natural sciences, named The Naturalist Bookshop, before a twenty-six-year career as a Boeing engineer with the Kennedy Space Center. Turning to architectural management, he also began with his sons a custom woodworking shop which, interestingly, created items for Disney World and Universal Studios.

Writing that his "love of nature and interaction with the environment" has been central to his life, Gleman shares tales from his mother's vegetable garden, the "profound and lasting effect" Rachel Carson's books imprinted on his life's worldview, and fascinating anecdotes from his careers, complete with photographs. Bits of poetry and quotations ranging from Carl Sagan to Winnie-the-Pooh enrich and populate his memoir. And along the journey, a positive and humble optimism prevails.

Gleman's book is a dedicated, wholesome, and deep proclamation of love and respect for Mother Nature. Often pausing to reflect upon the beauty of the ocean—particularly his family's beloved Folly Beach (in South Carolina) and her majestic aquatic life—Gleman provides rich, almost holy, consideration to the daily miracle of nature: the rising of the sun. "The sunrise provides a brand new canvas for us every day," writes Gleman, "and an opportunity to fill our minds and hearts with the beauty and wonder that surrounds us." Though not a book of poetry, much of his work reads like nature poetry, and this is an endearing hallmark of a gentleman for whom, growing up, "nature was always our playground."

— *JONAH MEYER*
US Review of Books (2023)

CONTENTS

DEDICATION

To my mother. Thank you for opening so many doors for me.

Acknowledgments

To my children, Adam and Adrian, who have added meaning and purpose to my life and made my journey much more interesting than I could ever have imagined.

To my mother, Jane, who always encouraged me to be the best I could be.

To my sisters and brothers, Mary, Stuart, Suzie, Mike, Pete, and Mark, who truly have been better than superheroes to me.

To all my teachers and mentors who enriched my life's journey. That helped me see the wonder of it all.

To the editorial group at Citi of Books.

And lastly, to my unfinished journey and yours. May it continue to provide love, joy, wonder, and peace as much as possible.

ABOUT THE AUTHOR

Jon Gleman was born just outside of Charleston, West Virginia. His family moved out of Charleston when he was a little more than one year old and made a couple of stops on their Southward journey before settling in Miami, Florida, when he was six years old. These stops and growing up in Miami in the 50s and 60s cemented his love of nature.

Jon has had several careers during his journey. He graduated with a BS in biology from the University of Miami and worked as an ecologist for many years in the 70s and 80s. During this time, he created and ran a small mail-order bookshop on natural sciences, The Naturalist Bookshop. In the mid-80s, he took a sharp turn in his career and worked for 26 years for Boeing at the Kennedy Space Center as an engineer and later a manager. He then took a management position for a large prestigious architecture and engineering firm in Orlando. During this time, he started a custom woodworking shop, Gleman and Sons Custom Woodworks, with his sons that provided many unique and extraordinary items for individuals as well as companies such as Walt Disney World and Universal Studios in Orlando.

Jon is retired now and is dedicating his journey to generating awareness on just how fortunate we are to be part of life here on our planet, Mother Earth, and the responsibilities we have to protect and preserve our home.

INTRODUCTION

No matter where you live on this planet there is one thing that we all need to agree on. It may be the most important decision mankind ever makes. Time is running out, and we won't get a second chance. Our planet, Mother Earth, is talking to us. At this point, she is imploring us to set things right, to stop defiling and polluting our home - the very planet we live on, along with all our earth-born companions. It has to stop, or life as we know it will change for the worse. It already is.

One thing that has been a part of me since early childhood is my connection to nature and the world around me. In many ways, being a part of nature, studying nature, and communicating with it has been my life's work. And I believe that it is time now to share my journey with you.

I have a degree in biology from the University of Miami, and I have worked as an ecologist for many years. I also have an extensive background in electrical controls engineering. One thing that electrical controls engineering will teach you is that feedback is critical. Mother Earth has been giving us constant feedback on the issues we humans have created for our planet.

Jane Goodall (one of my heroes), in her latest book, The Book of Hope, A Survival Guide for Trying Times, shared a series of dialogues with co-author Douglas Abrams, in which she gives her take on the grave issues we face today.

"Doug, I honestly believe we can turn things around. But – yes there is a but – we must get together and act now."

My hope is that you will find these stories of my journey entertaining and enlightening. They will inspire you to do all that you can to connect with our earth-born companions and to restore, preserve, and protect our beautiful home, Mother Earth.

Passage 1

Jon's Journey Begins

"A beginning is a very delicate time"

— Frank Herbert — Dune

My love of nature and my interaction with the environment have been central to my life for as long as I can remember. I've been around a while. I grew up in the 50s and 60s, so this journey is not so much a beginning for me as it is the beginning of me sharing my stories about my interaction, understanding, and love of nature. It is a story about that connection with our incredible planet, Mother Earth, and all living beings around us (including our fellow plants and animals).

"For most of history, man has had to fight nature to survive; in this century, he is beginning to realize that, in order to survive, he must protect it." —Jacques-Yves Cousteau. Cousteau is one of my childhood heroes. He brought to life the beauty and wonders of life under the sea for all of us and helped increase our understanding of our home, Mother Earth.

I worked as an engineer for a contractor for NASA at the Kennedy Space Center as part of our space program. The Voyager 1 space probe took a photo of Earth from approximately 3.7 billion miles away. The Earth shows up in that photo as a pale blue dot. Carl Sagan points out that "To my mind, there is perhaps, no better demonstration of the folly of human conceits than his distant image of our tiny world. To me, it underscores our responsibility to deal more kindly and compassionately with one another and to preserve and cherish the pale blue dot, the only home we've ever known."

There can be no more important endeavor for mankind now than to do just that. Preserve and protect our home, Mother Earth.

You are here

My First Garden

"Life begins the day you start a garden"

— *Chinese Proverb*

When I was in 2nd grade, I asked my mother if I could grow a vegetable garden. She had often talked, from time to time, about her garden on the farm where she had grown up. I wanted to grow my own vegetables like my mother.

My mother bought some radish seeds, and we made a small vegetable garden plot in our backyard and planted the seeds. Within two or three days, the radish seeds sprouted, and before I knew it, I had my first harvest. I've had a vegetable garden of some size every year since then. My mother literally planted the seed in my mind and helped me cultivate it. It has turned into a lifelong endeavor that has given me a great deal of joy and a sense of accomplishment. It has also provided countless bushels of fresh, organically-grown vegetables and fruit for me, my family, and friends. Along the way, it has also taught me that just like a garden needs to be cultivated to produce the best and most healthy vegetables, our lives need cultivating just as well to be the best we can be and to help others be their best.

"The love of gardening is a seed once sown that never dies."

— *Gertrude Jekyll*

When my older sister learned of my vegetable garden, she told me about organic gardening. She sent me a copy of 'Organic Gardening' by Rodale Press, and I have been an organic gardener ever since. It just made and, to this day, makes so much sense to me. The food we eat should be as pure and healthy as possible, just like the air we breathe and the water we drink. Not just for us either. For all our fellow plants and animals. We all deserve this at the very least.

"Remember that children, marriages, and flower gardens reflect the kind of care they get."

— H. Jackson Brown, Jr.

I think the same rules that apply to cultivating a vegetable garden apply to life as well.

1.) A vegetable garden requires constant attention and loving care.

So do relationships.

2.) A vegetable garden is dynamic. Its needs change on an almost daily basis. The weather, the soil (too dry, too wet), weeding, and even just talking to the plants are some indispensable needs for plants. I make it a point to do all this and more. I always have.

Similarly, our relationships needs change and nourishment on a daily basis as well. All the things that apply to your garden apply to your relationships too. Even if some only metaphorically.

3.) Heading off problems before they become too big. It is important to keep a good eye on what's happening in the garden. As I said, I talk to the plants on a regular basis and in the process, in a way, they talk back to me. I notice things that are going well and things that can be potential problems. I survey the garden regularly and take corrective actions when needed.

Communication is a key element in any relationship.

4.) Cultivating your garden takes time. It requires a commitment to take the time needed. There are no shortcuts.

Taking the time and making the time is another key element in any relationship.

5.) The rewards make all the effort worth it many times over. A bountiful harvest of fresh vegetables is your reward. There is nothing like a home-grown tomato.

There is no price that can be placed on a loving, caring relationship.

Isn't it funny how a few seeds planted in a seven year's old mind can sprout into such a bountiful harvest of life's lessons? My mother certainly knew what she was doing. And I thought I was just planting a few radish seeds in my first vegetable garden.

Opening Doors

"The more clearly we can focus our attention on the wonders and realities of the universe about us, the less taste we shall have for destruction."

— Rachel Carson

One of my childhood heroes is Rachel Carson. I remember once when I was around ten years old, my mother and I were in the book section of a department store, and as she looked at books, I found a copy of Rachel Carson's *"The Sea Around Us."* I sat down and started to read it. She had me on the first page. What a wondrous world it opened up for me!

Much to my surprise and uncontainable joy, my mother bought it for me. It was the hard copy edition and relatively expensive, but my mom bought it, and I couldn't wait to get home and read it from cover to cover.

It had a profound and lasting effect on me. After reading it, I decided I wanted to become a marine biologist.

Rachael Carson, herself, was a marine biologist. She worked at the U. S. Bureau of Fisheries, which later turned into the U. S. Fish and Wildlife Service. But her writings are what she is particularly known for.

She published three books on the sea; "Under the Sea-Wind," "The Sea Around Us," which became a bestseller and won a national book award, and "The Edge of the Sea." These books not only help to increase our understanding of oceans but also instill love and appreciation for them. They helped cement my love of the ocean and the world around us. So much so, as I said, it was due to her books that I decided to become a biologist to learn as much as I could about our incredible planet and all the life on it.

"Those who contemplate the beauty of the earth find reserves of strength that will endure as long as life lasts. There is something infinitely healing

in the repeated refrains of nature-the assurance that dawn comes after night, and spring after winter."

— *Rachael Carson*

In 1962, Rachael Carson published "Silent Spring." This book helped in spreading awareness worldwide of the serious issues we were and still are creating with the use of pesticides and other related chemicals on our planet and the seriously negative effects pollution has on the planet and all living things.

As an organic gardener and a biologist/ecologist, since I was seven years old, her writings have deeply inspired me to this day. Her books have allowed me to appreciate the magnificent gift we all share every day to live on our beautiful planet Earth and be a part of Mother Nature.

I shall remain grateful to my mother and Rachel Carson for turning a simple shopping trip into a life-changing event for me. Thank you both for opening that door.

I have been very fortunate throughout my journey to have people open doors for me and to make it possible for me to expand my horizons and observe things from a different perspective because they took the time to open a door for me. I will write about those experiences further in this book.

"If a child is to keep alive his (her) inborn sense of wonder, he (she) needs the companionship of at least one adult who can share it, rediscovering with him (her) the joy, excitement, and mystery of the world we live in."

— *Rachel Carson.*

PASSAGE 2

$\longrightarrow \longleftarrow$

A Single Step

"A journey of a thousand miles begins with a single step"

— *Lao - Tzu*

I have had several careers during my journey. When I was a child, my brothers and I would seize every opportunity to spend some time in the fields and woods near our house. We went fishing whenever we could. We loved being outdoors. So I think it's only natural (pun intended) that I went to college at the University of Miami and got a BS in Biology, thus becoming a biologist, an ecologist, and a naturalist. After graduating college, I worked as an ecologist for many years in the '70s and '80s.

Benthic Study at Crystal River Florida

"In wildness is the preservation of the world."

— *Henry David Thoreau*

Next, I created and ran a small mail-order bookshop on natural sciences. This was in the mid-'70s through the mid-'80s. I contemplated expanding the bookshop to sell items related to nature other than books but eventually decided on a different career path instead. It may be of some interest that Amazon started in 1995. I would say I was a little ahead of my time, but I certainly did not have a vision for mail-order products on a scale like Amazon is selling.

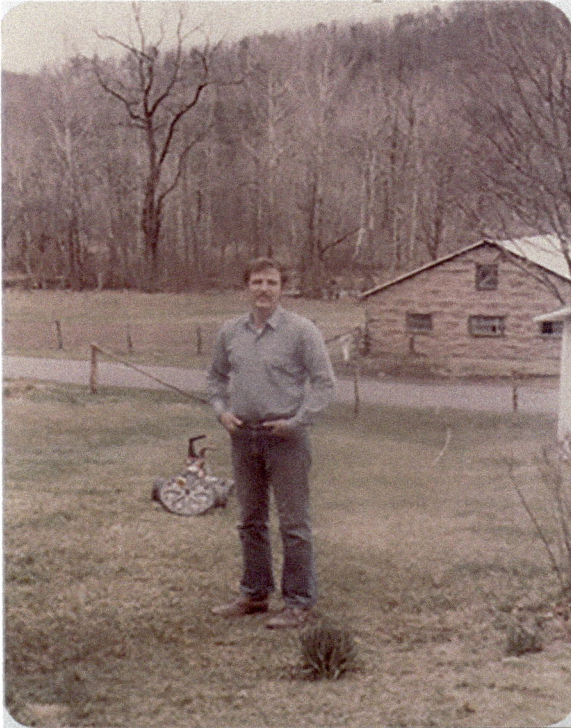

The Naturalist Bookshop Rock Oak West Virginia

In the mid-'80s, I took an entirely new path and started work in electrical controls design for a contractor for NASA at the Kennedy Space Center. This was a totally new endeavor for me that provided many new challenges. It was also a great opportunity to learn new things and be part of something much bigger than myself. This was around the time in our space program when work was just starting on the support efforts needed for our Space Station. It was very exciting work, indeed.

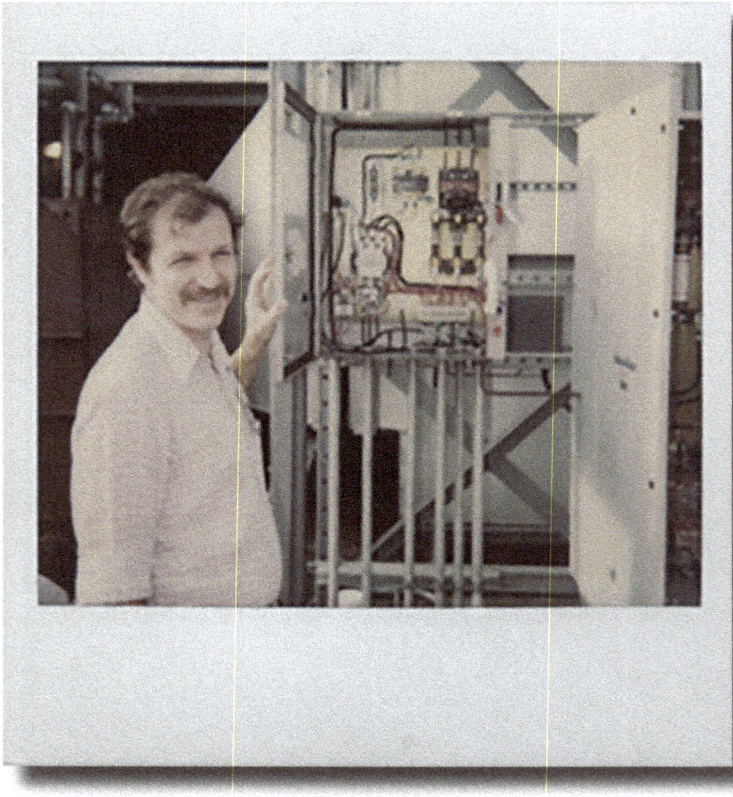

Hypergol Scrubber Control Panel Kennedy Space Center

They didn't know what title to give me at first with my degree in biology, so they settled on a Technical Specialist. However, I worked my way up the engineering ladder quickly and went progressively from an associate engineer to engineer, then to senior engineer and finally principal engineer for Boeing, and then into management. I worked at the Kennedy Space Center for 26 years.

Speaking of the Kennedy Space Center on May 25, 1961, President Kennedy addressed a joint session of Congress and proposed the outrageous goal of landing a man on the moon before the end of the decade.

The Irish writer Frank O'Connor wrote about how as a boy, he and his friends would challenge one another by tossing their caps over a wall that seemed too high to climb. Then, in order to retrieve their caps, they had no choice but to follow.

In his dedication speech at the Aerospace Medical Health Center in San Antonio on November 21, 1963, the day before he was assassinated, President Kennedy referenced this story and concluded his speech with:

"This nation has tossed its cap over the wall of space and we have no choice but to follow it."

— *John F. Kennedy*

After my passage at the Kennedy Space Center, I moved on to a management position for a large, prestigious Architecture and Engineering company in Orlando. I wore multiple hats there. I was hired as the Manager of Quality Assurance but soon started and oversaw their project management program. I instilled a total quality management approach to their work products like that used at the Kennedy Space Center that was managed through the project managers.

"It's not enough to do your best; you must know what to do and then do your best."

— *W. Edwards Deming*

During this time, my sons and I started a custom woodworking shop. What started out as a backyard pole barn that we closed in and furnished with three pieces of woodworking equipment has grown into a thriving custom woodworking and metalworking shop in a 53,000 square foot facility over the years. Many of the pieces are crafted from reclaimed and salvaged lumber. For instance, boards removed from a 100-year-old barn or building or lumber milled from cypress logs submerged in a river for a hundred years. To this day Gleman & Sons Custom Woodworks provides many unique and extraordinary crafted items for individuals as well as companies such as Disney, Universal Studios, Darden Restaurants, and Foxtail Coffee Shops.

Gleman & Sons Custom Woodworks Handiwork

"Education is the most powerful weapon which you can use to change the world."

—*Nelson Mandela*

So let's see if we can change the world a little bit together and hopefully have a little fun doing it.

Let's all throw our cap over the wall!

Use it up...

Growing up in the fifties, the war, WWII, was still all too fresh on everyone's mind. I remember my parents and grandmother talking about food rationing. Other things were simply not available that were used in the manufacturing of our military equipment and to support our troops and our allies' troops.

There were some stories about the war itself but not a lot. One of my American history teachers was in tank battles in Europe. He never talked about specifics, just that there is a price to be paid for our freedom at times and that we are very fortunate to have the freedom we share in this country.

My grandmother had a saying she would repeat to us on a regular basis. "Use it up, wear it out, make it last, or do without." This was based no doubt on the WWII slogan of "use it up, wear it out, make it do, or do without." We are certainly a long way from the '50s and WWII, but I think this advice holds true today as much as it did then. We (I include myself here) just don't practice it as much as we should.

My first car was a 1951 Chevy pickup. It was in pretty good shape when I got it in 1974. The engine needed a valve job, but otherwise, it ran well. My older brothers Stuart and Mike helped me in taking it apart and cleaning it, which was the first thing to do, of course. I could literally stand in the engine well on either side of the motor while I worked on it. It had a few quirks, like the windshield wipers. They ran off the vacuum system of the engine so that when you would accelerate, they would slow down to a crawl, and then when you let off the gas, they would slap the rain like crazy, going three times their normal speed. In Miami, this mostly was not a problem, but when you would go up an overpass, they slowed down to a crawl, and it could get a little hard to see. Going down the overpass, I was sure the wipers were going to fly off the windshield. I eventually replaced them with electric motor wipers. Safer, but not nearly as much fun.

The thing is, my first car was twenty-three years old when I got it. I ran it for several years before I passed it on to someone else who would put many more years of use on it. For me fixing up that old truck was a labor of love. With all its quirks, it had a personality, and, of course, it had that old fabled pickup truck look. The other thing is I was putting into practice the advice my grandmother gave to all of my brothers and sisters and me so many years before. I believe no better advice can be found today than "Use it up, wear it out, make it last, or do without."

Born out of necessity during WWII, it's a piece of advice that, if followed today, can help anyone and literally the whole world in so many ways. People need to have a sense of purpose and a sense of accomplishment. Figuring out how to fix something and making it last does just that. And reusing something, when it makes sense, helps keep our beautiful planet cleaner and safer, and more livable for all of us. Plants, animals, and people. A hard-to-beat combination.

Sea Fever

One of my mother's favorite poems was Sea Fever by John Masefield. John Masefield was an English poet, writer, and was Poet Laureate of England from 1930 until 1967.

Sea Fever

I must go down to the seas again, to the lonely sea and the sky,

And all I ask is a tall ship and a star to steer her by,

And the wheel's kick and the wind's song and the white sail's shaking,

And a grey mist on the sea's face, and a gray dawn breaking.

I must go down to the seas again, for the call of the running tide

Is a wild call and a clear call that may not be denied;

And all I ask is a windy day with the white clouds flying,

And the flung spray and the blown spume, and the sea-gulls crying.

I must go down to the seas again, to the vagrant gypsy life,

To the gull's way and the whale's way where the wind's like a whetted knife;

And all I ask is a merry yarn from a laughing fellow-rover

And quiet sleep and a sweet dream when the long trick's over.

I grew up in South Florida and have lived in Florida for the better part of my life. So being around the sea and spending time on the ocean has been a natural part of my life—something I have enjoyed immensely. So much so that I planned on becoming a marine biologist. I got sidetracked in college a little and became an ecologist instead. But much of my studies on how plants and animals interact with their environment involved marine life. However, there is so much more to the sea than you can possibly study. There is a lure that pulls you in, a call, to quote John Masefield.

Some time back, my wife and I had the opportunity to spend an evening on the sea on our very dear friend's boat. There is something about the salt breeze and waves that soothe the soul. A connection that cannot be denied. And in the morning, I was fortunate enough to view the beautiful golden yellow sunrise.

"The Triumph of Life" by Percy B. Shelley

Swift as a spirit hastening to his task

Of glory & of good, the Sun sprang forth

Rejoicing in his splendor, & the mask

of darkness fell from the awakened Earth.

Sunrise on the ocean

So, what is this allure of the sea? Well, for one thing, the sea is usually blue or green or turquoise—all soothing colors. The blue color gives a sense of coolness and calms the mind. Research shows that it is the world's (people in the world) favorite color. That's interesting to me because so much of the world is covered in blue water, and of course, blue sky. Green is restful to the eye and provides a sense of balance - a sense of peace. Turquoise, as you might expect, seems to follow along the lines of blue and green as far as the feelings people associate with it. It also may instill an increase in energy.

Is it any wonder then that the sea holds such a spell over us?

Passage 3

Big Brothers

As I mentioned in the introduction, I was number six out of seven children in my family. I had four brothers and two sisters. My brothers and sisters were very helpful in my upbringing, cared greatly for me, and kept a good loving eye on me.

When I was eleven years old, I noticed two of my older brothers were making money mowing lawns for our neighbors. I talked with my friend about it, and we decided we would mow lawns to make some extra money as well. However, there was just one problem - we didn't have a lawnmower. I did have an old mower at the house that didn't run, though. So, I talked to my eldest brother, Stuart, about what my friend and I were planning to do. We found the lawnmower and looked it over. He told me that he could get it running, but it would take some time and work.

Consequently, Stuart took me under his wing and explained to me what needed to be done. The first thing was to take the mower completely apart and clean it. He told me to make sure to label the parts and the order they go back together, or our project might get more interesting than we planned on.

Once we got past the accumulation of dirt and grease and grime and the dents and dings from years of use, the mower seemed to be in good shape once again. Stuart thought that other than some tender loving care, it probably just needed new points and a condenser. It turned out he was right, and for good measure, I gave the mower a new paint job — a white motor with a tan body from the leftover paint in the utility room.

Arnold and I were now finally in the lawn mowing business! We charged the going rate for the day, $1.50 for a regular lawn and $2.00 for a corner yard, which was big money in those days. A Snickers or a Royal Palm soda cost a nickel back then, and you could get into the movie theater for thirty-five cents. If there was edging or other work of that sort, it was decided that my brothers would take care of that. We were set.

"Sometimes being a brother is even better than being a superhero"

— *Marc Brown.*

Certainly, you can imagine that my brothers and sisters were better than superheroes to me, and I hope I was as well to them. I think an advantage of having a lot of brothers and sisters is the bonds that form. When I talked to Stuart about wanting to mow lawns to make some extra money like my brothers were, he didn't put me off by saying that he had his own stuff to do. Instead, he took me under his wing and showed me the right way to fix something. He didn't do the work himself. To this day, I follow his formula and mentoring style. It wasn't just about making an old lawnmower work again. It was about teaching a younger brother how to make life work. It was about helping someone else, about teamwork, about caring.

I have so many stories about my brothers and sisters to share with you. In many ways, they have molded me into the person I am today. I could never ask for a better bunch of "better than superheroes" to be a part of my life.

Sitting on the Cactus and Howling

My mother had a saying when I was growing up that helped my siblings and me to focus. Whenever we complained to her about something that had happened to us, something that was going on around us that we didn't agree with, or we just wanted things to be different, she would say, "So, are you going to sit on the cactus and howl?"

Thus, it didn't take too long for us to figure out that although my mother was very interested in what we had to say, what we were complaining about, or what we thought needed changing, she expected us to do something about it. Take the problem at hand, the issue, the situation, and do something positive to make it better, to fix it, to change it.

As I have traveled on my journey of life, the advice that my mother passed on to me at a very young age has served me well. And as with most guidance that someone passes on to you, I took it, made it my own, and added to it.

As time passes, new phrases develop within our language. When I was a child, what we would have characterized as a situation or an issue has at times turned into "It is what it is!" Excuse me?!

I remember some time back when I first heard the term "It is what it is" I was working at the Kennedy Space Center, managing a design project for Ground Support Equipment (GSE). One thing about the space program is that it loves acronyms. During a discussion of a particular parameter for the project, the engineer in charge of the area informed the team that we could not do what we had planned. That was that, and "It is what it is." I'm sure the team saw the look of surprise and disbelief on my face. Well, I told the team we would have to change it and make it something that would do what we needed to be done. After this, I thought back on what my mother had taught us. Saying something can't be changed or accepting something that needs changing is just another way of sitting on the cactus and howling. I always do my best to take the problem at hand, the "It is what it is," and do something positive to make it better, to fix it, to change it exactly as my mother had taught me.

Along the way, I have taught myself a trick that works well for me when I'm having a little trouble figuring out just how to move forward with the problem at hand. I call it making the problem change colors. Take a step back and try to develop a wider perspective of the problem. Stand it on its head. Look at it from different angles. If nothing else, change the way you look at it, and that may help you to move forward with a solution. But this is a subject for another time.

Another thing I have learned along the way. Don't let problems and issues pile up. There are always going to be new problems and issues that come up on your journey. Focus. Take them head-on. In a positive way, put them to rest so that you can focus and move on in your journey.

So, are you going to sit on the cactus and howl?

What In The World?

There are a few everyday life things that have changed since I was a kid. Well, actually, a lot of everyday life things have changed since I was a kid. But I mean material things. I thought it might be fun to reminisce a little about this. Also, reading about these things might also make you stop and think a little bit about the things that we take for granted today.

Phones

I know I am really dating myself here, but when I was very young, we had one phone for the entire house. That's right! One phone. It was a rotary phone and a landline, of course. For perspective, the first public use of mobile phones happened in 1973. Not only was there only one phone in the house until then, but it was also a party line. For those of you who don't know what a party line is, most of you, I imagine, it was a local telephone circuit that was shared by several customers. So when you picked up the phone to make a call that is with your parents' permission, of course, sometimes there was someone else already talking on the other side of the phone. The thing to do at that time was to hang up and try to make your call later. That's what we were taught and how we used our phones. I think sometimes people didn't hang up and got a good source of neighborhood gossip, no doubt.

Party Line Rules

In the mid-'60s, we got a touch-tone phone. Also, the party line was gone by this time. But that doesn't mean the old rotary phone was thrown out too. As I have written about it before, my grandmother's saying, "Use it up, wear it out, make it last, or do without," definitely applied here. I'll talk about that another time. Thus, we upgraded to a touch-tone phone and eventually to one with an extra-long cord, so we did not have to stand in the kitchen to talk on the phone. We could actually walk all the way to the dining room to have a phone conversation. The phone rules still applied—no long-distance calls. You paid extra for them. And, you still had to have your parents' permission to make a call.

As you can see, phones have advanced a long way from when I was a kid; they really are not phones anymore but computers that can be used as a phone when needed. I wonder what Alexander Graham Bell would think? And, as far as the demise of the party line and its role in spreading neighborhood gossip is concerned, I feel certain that people came up with other means of hearing and conveying the gossip.

"When one door closes another door opens; but we so often look so long and so regretfully upon the closed door, that we do not see the ones which open for us."

— *Alexander Graham Bell*

You know there are many other material things that we used and took for granted when I was a kid that have long since been replaced. I'll talk about them in some future stories of my journey. I'm sure it will be fun.

PASSAGE 4

If You're Skipping, You're Smiling

Along the way in my journey, I've figured out there are certain things you do in life that just go together. There are just some things you do in life without even trying, and before you know it, they are a lot of fun. That's how it is with skipping. I've noticed that if you're skipping, you're smiling. You just can't help it. You start skipping, and then without even noticing it, you're smiling. It's, I think, a natural by-product of skipping. One thing leads to another without you thinking about it or trying to make it happen. It just happens. Pretty cool, I think.

Speaking of smiles. Did you know that when you smile, your facial muscles contract in a way that it, in turn, sends a signal back to your brain, increasing your level of happy hormones or endorphins? When our brain feels happy, we smile, and when we smile, our brain feels happy. It's a pretty good arrangement, I think. In fact, it makes me smile just to think about it.

Smiles are contagious. That's right! Studies have shown that people smile when they see someone smiling at them. I'm sure you have noticed this. One smile begets another. How can you beat that?

Smiling is our first facial expression. Between six and eight weeks, babies develop a social smile—an intentional gesture of warmth.

Smiling can relieve stress and make you feel better. It relieves physical tension and stress. Smiling has been shown to reduce your body's stress response. It lowers heart rate and blood pressure.

Smiling can boost your immune system. Smiling or laughing activates molecules in your brain that fight stress and illnesses.

A smile is the most recognized facial expression.

"If you smile at me, I will understand, cause that is something everybody everywhere does in the same language."

— *Wooden Ships Crosby Stills Nash*

Yes, there is a downside to it too. Smiling will cause smile lines on your face, but that isn't necessarily a bad thing, in my opinion. Those small lines at the corner of your eyes are a symbol of the happiness you have experienced through life.

As Jimmy Buffett says:

"Wrinkles only go where the smiles have been."

— *Barefoot Children.*

So next time you find yourself skipping, take a moment and check and see if you're smiling.

Something Desired

I first read the prose poem "Desiderata" when I was in college in the early 1970s. It was very popular then. It really struck a chord with me. It is something I have strived to follow my entire life, even before I became aware of its message.

I passed it along to my sons and gave them a framed copy at graduation.

I don't know how to improve upon it.

Desiderata by Max Ehrmann

Go placidly amid the noise and haste,
and remember what peace there may be in silence.
As far as possible without surrender
be on good terms with all persons.
Speak your truth quietly and clearly;
and listen to others,
even the dull and the ignorant;
they, too, have their story.

Avoid loud and aggressive persons;
they are vexations to the spirit.
If you compare yourself with others,
you may become vain and bitter;
for always there will be greater and lesser persons than yourself.
Enjoy your achievements as well as your plans.

Keep interested in your own career, however humble;
it is a real possession in the changing fortunes of time.
Exercise caution in your business affairs;

for the world is full of trickery.
But let this not blind you to what virtue there is;
many persons strive for high ideals;
and everywhere life is full of heroism.

Be yourself.
Especially, do not feign affection.
Neither be cynical about love;
for in the face of all aridity and disenchantment
It is as perennial as the grass.

Take kindly the counsel of the years,
gracefully surrendering the things of youth.
Nurture strength of spirit to shield you in sudden misfortune.
But do not distress yourself with dark imaginings.
Many fears are born of fatigue and loneliness.
Beyond a wholesome discipline,
be gentle with yourself.

You are a child of the universe,
no less than the trees and the stars;
you have a right to be here.
And whether or not it is clear to you,
no doubt the universe is unfolding as it should.

Therefore be at peace with God,
whatever you conceive Him to be,
and whatever your labors and aspirations,
in the noisy confusion of life, keep peace with your soul.

With all its sham, drudgery, and broken dreams,
It is still a beautiful world.
Be cheerful.
Strive to be happy.

Morning Song

When I wake up in the morning or shortly after, I have a morning song in my head. Often I start humming it or singing it softly to myself. This has been going on almost for as long as I can remember. I thought that everybody had their own morning song until I found out a few years ago that's not the case. In fact, I don't know of anyone else who has a morning song. I'm OK with that. I like having a morning song. I even like the morning song from "Friends" and sing it from time to time in the morning, much to my family's consternation.

https://youtu.be/S_PGP5QiIss

I do wonder at times why a particular song is going through my head on a particular morning, but I try not to overthink it. I rather like to enjoy these moments. My morning song this morning is "Breathe In, Breathe Out, Move On" by Jimmy Buffett and Matt Betton (a drummer and songwriter in the Coral Reefer Band).

https://youtu.be/c-GUBkymgzw

"Breathe In, Breathe Out, Move On" was included on Jimmy's 2006 album *Take the Weather with You* as a tribute to victims of Hurricane Katrina. Again I don't know why this is my morning song today, but I think it is good advice. With so much happening in our world and our lives these days, whenever possible, just take a couple of deep breaths, rewind, and move on.

PASSAGE 5

Folly Beach Remembered – Part I

I was born in Nitro, West Virginia, just outside of its capital city, Charleston. We lived across the street from the Kanawha River and very close to the Union Carbide plant where both of my parents worked. We moved from there when I was a little more than a year old. However, while growing up, I heard the stories my parents and older siblings would tell about the time we spent there.

The reason we moved, I think, is pretty interesting. Periodically, a tank at the plant would explode and break some of the windows in the house. The company would then pay to replace them, and everybody went on about their business. Then one time, an explosion was bad enough to damage the foundation of the house. My parents used the money that was paid for the repair to move. So that is how we managed to move to Miami. The stay in Miami was fairly short-lived. Even though I was very young and don't remember much, I remember where we moved next very well. It was to Folly Beach, South Carolina.

The house at Folly Beach was two stories tall and sat just across the road from a beautiful white beach. I had never seen a beach before we moved there. I remember the white sand as far as you could see, with endless waves, two of which never seemed to look the same. There were tidal pools, seagulls, pelicans, sand dunes, and a blue sky. Every day was a brand new adventure. Especially if you have a flock of young brothers, it literally opened up a whole new world for you.

I was still very young, but I remember running up and down the beach with my brothers and sister, Suzie. We would splash the waves and explore the tidal pools. We set up a small goldfish aquarium in the living room. We would put small crabs and shrimp in the tank along with some small fishes and, occasionally, a seahorse, too, if we were lucky enough to find one.

One of my brothers bought a box kite and a ball of string. There was always a breeze on the beach, and we took turns flying a kite. We figured out that we could also make a box kite like the one we had so that each one of us would have our own kite to fly. We did, and we all had great fun with our kites. If anyone tells you to go and fly a kite, take them up on it. It's a very calming, relaxing, and just plain fun thing to do.

It's hard to imagine a better setting for my siblings and me to have adventures happen than our time spent on Folly Beach in the early '50s. Nature was our playground.

As Winnie the Pooh says:

"We didn't realize we were making memories, we just knew we were having fun."

Folly Beach Remembered - Part II

My family moved to Folly Beach when I was just four years old. We only lived there for a little over a year, but it was totally worth it. It was a great place to find adventure for my brothers and me.

"As soon as I saw you I knew an adventure was going to happen."

—*Winnie the Pooh*

One day during our time at Folly Beach, we were enjoying the freedom of life on the ocean as kids; my brothers decided they wanted some candy. There was a pier that was somewhat of a hike to the north. A small general store there had candy. This time I got to go with them. I bought a fireball – a favorite of mine ever since that day. It cost a penny.

At the age of four, it was my very first purchase. On the way home, we found a herring seagull with an injured wing. We took it and brought it home. Our parents let us keep it to try and nurse it back to health. We made a cage for it in the backyard. My brother, Pete, and I would catch a variety of small fish for it in the tidal pools at the beach. I don't remember what we named it, but I don't think it cared what we called it as long as we brought some fish for it. Our dog, Scotch, a beautiful, happy, and friendly Bernese Mountain dog, showed great interest in our seagull. The cage was built off the ground, and Scotch would lie under it during the day. I'm sure he was just protecting it. After some time, our seagull seemed to have healed. We had a little ceremony on the beach and let it go. It didn't fly away but ran to join the other gulls on the beach.

One brisk spring morning, my mother called us all to go down to the beach. There was a strong wind blowing, the waves were thundering on the shore, and there was a mist in the air. A little further out from the waves was a sight to behold.

There was an endless stream of dolphins leaping through the air. They were all headed north. There literally must have been thousands. We watched in utter amazement for what seemed like an hour, and they were still going. What an absolutely breathtaking, beautiful, and awe-inspiring sight! Something I shall never forget.

Folly Beach was like that!

Folly Beach Remembered – Part III

I have written a couple of stories now about the time my family and I spent in Folly Beach, South Carolina. I wrote about things that happened and events I remember as a four-year-old. As I was growing older, I was just starting to really connect with my older brothers and sisters, with my parents, and with the world around me, i.e., nature. In the '50s, Folly Beach was one of the perfect places to experience a memorable childhood.

The endless beach provided not just a playground for my siblings and me but also the opportunity to be totally immersed in nature from sun-up to sun-down – and that's precisely what we did. We enjoyed every waking minute spent on the beach or the woods behind our house. Every day was spent soaking up nature, engaging in the beautiful natural world around us, and learning just how we all get along, i.e., people, plants, and animals, on this planet. It only makes sense that when I grew up, I became an Ecologist (a scientist who studies how animals and plants interact with their environment and each other). I already was one, thanks to my time spent at Folly Beach.

"Look deep into nature, and then you will understand everything better."

— *Albert Einstein*

My earliest memories in life are from my time spent there. Not just of the natural world around me but of connecting and growing with my family. These things made the time I spent there full of beautiful memories.

"The child is father of the man."

— *William Wordsworth*

From

My Heart Leaps Up

My heart leaps up when I behold

A rainbow in the sky:

So was it when my life began;

So is it now I am a man;

So be it when I shall grow old,

Or let me die!

The Child is father of the Man;

And I could wish my days to be

Bound each to each by natural piety.

I don't think of a better summary of my life from the very beginning of my memories to now can be written. I think we all will benefit, as will Mother Earth and all our "earth-born companions," if we only have natural piety for the world around us.

PASSAGE 6

So, Tell Me Again, Why Did I Become a Long Distance Runner?

One time in grade school, I read an article about the Boston Marathon, and for some reason, I decided that I wanted to take part in it. I can't exactly explain why maybe there was a sense that it would be quite an accomplishment to finish it. Something I could look back at the finish line after I had crossed it and say to myself, "There you go, I did that!" Little did I know that this time, instead of a person opening a door for me, it was a thing, an event.

My brothers and I were very active in sports in high school – be it football, wrestling, or track. Then later in college, it was lacrosse. We were all fairly accomplished at sports, but that's a story for another time.

When I graduated high school, I wanted to do something that would help keep me in shape. I decided that I would take up long-distance running. My brother, Stuart, thought that was a great idea. He had been on University of Miami cross country track team, and we started training together.

We were very fortunate because we had many places where we could train long distances right from where we lived. For instance, after running along a couple of fairly safe roads, we came to the bike trail on Old Cutler Road; from there, you could run to Matheson Hammock Park or Fairchild Tropical Gardens for a "short" six-mile run, or head north to Cocoplum Circle and beyond depending on how far you wanted your training run to be. Always a beautiful run, even in the rain. I always enjoyed running in the rain as long as there was no lightning.

Believe it or not, when we started, running shoes were not really available at stores in the country. That didn't matter to us so much because we didn't have money to buy them anyway. We really were starving (not exactly) college kids.

My parents passed away when I was in high school. So, Stuart and I ran barefoot. That's right! Our first few years of long-distance running were done sans shoes. We didn't think anything of it. Most of the time, it worked. There were the occasional blisters, but we built up calluses quickly and were fortunate not to step on anything sharp.

Maybe now is a good time to provide a short marathon race history. The marathon is a long-distance race of 26.2 miles. The event was instituted in commemoration of the fabled run of the Greek soldier Pheidippides, a messenger from the Battle of Marathon to Athens, who reported the victory of the Athenians over the Persians in the battle of marathon.

When the modern Olympics began in 1896 in Athens, Greece, the organizers were looking for a great popularizing event, recalling the glory of ancient Greece. The idea of a marathon race came from Michel Breal, who wanted the event to feature in the first modern Olympic Games in 1896.

The journey of Pheidippides from Marathon to Athens also inspired the first Boston Marathon on April 19, 1897. The Boston Marathon is the world's oldest annual marathon and is also notable for allowing women to compete in 1972 when the first Olympic marathon for women wasn't held until 1984. I'll talk about the Boston Marathon in another story.

Our first marathon was the Space Coast Marathon in Melbourne, Florida, in December 1971. It was also the first Space Coast Marathon, now in its 50th year. Marathon races were different back then. There were a total of 61 starters.

Stuart finished, but I did not. My knees gave way, and after 21 miles, I was done. My knees swelled up to the size of grapefruits, and of course, my feet were covered with blisters. But it was my knees that were the problem. They slowly got better, but I have to admit I took the elevator to the second floor of the University of Miami library for a few days – something I had never done before. Going up and downstairs is good training for long-distance running, I believe.

Stuart helped with my knee problem. I was running flat footed. I needed to run more on the balls of my feet and the outside edge. I have never had another knee issue once I started running this way. Now running barefoot might have contributed to my knee problems as well. We solved that problem soon after our first marathon. How? That's also a story for another day.

After the marathon, the blisters on my feet and my grapefruit knees were not my biggest problem. I was very disappointed that I didn't complete something I had started to accomplish. I'm glad to say I went on to run many more marathons successfully and that I have learned to deal with failure much better. To learn from it and turn it into a positive experience.

The Total Eclipse of the Sun, 1972

The most extraordinary thing happened during the summer of 1972, and I was fortunate enough to experience it. The memory of that day is just as fresh to me today as the day it happened. One of those childhood events leads to "long, long thoughts."

My brother, Stuart, and I decided to travel to Prince Edward Island, Canada to witness the solar eclipse and to take some photographs. Stuart was a graduate student at the University of Miami Physics Department at the time, so he wanted to collect data on the eclipse. We flew up to New York and then drove to Prince Edward Island. The trip itself was quite an adventure for me. I had never been to New York City or Canada.

Photo Stuart took of the 1972 total eclipse of the Sun

We drove through some beautiful countryside to get to Prince Edward Island from New York City. It was quite a change of scenery for a boy from South Florida. Mountains, hills, deciduous forests, lakes, streams, and bays. Quite a change of scenery.

We took the ferry across Northumberland Strait and went to the campsite set by the University of Miami expedition on the island's north side. It was set on the edge of the North Atlantic Ocean. There was a small cliff of about 10 feet to the beach. There are no cliffs to the beach in Miami, just a very gentle slope. All of these things were new to me.

Eclipse Campsite – Prince Edward Island

To the south of us was a large wetland area with many wetland types of birds. This was to be an important ingredient of my eclipse experience, believe it or not.

The morning of the eclipse was a bit concerning. It was completely overcast. You could not see the sky because of the thick cloud cover. As the time for the eclipse approached, our concerns grew. There was no break in the cloud cover to be seen. Then with only 20 to 30 minutes to go until the eclipse, the sky opened up. The clouds cleared away, and the eclipse started. As the moon covered more and more of the sun, it became darker and darker. The moon's ever-changing silhouette across the sun was fascinating to watch.

Getting ready for the eclipse

The eclipse was absolutely fascinating. I was taking color photos but took a little time to look around. There was a 360 degrees sunset. It was orange and red and beautiful. As the sunset started, all the egrets and herons in the marsh thought it was nighttime and started flying home to roost. There were quite a few of them. When the sun came back out, they flew back to the marsh. A very interesting observation for a biology major. I was, of course, thinking the whole trip about the eclipse, and as the eclipse unfolded, how it affected people. It turns out it affects the whole planet, including plants and animals.

Color photo I took of the 1972 total eclipse of the Sun

After the eclipse, we had dinner at the camp, and everyone talked about what we had just witnessed. The next morning we took the ferry back to the mainland, and on the drive back to the city, we saw a moose next to a lake near the road. We stopped and said hello. The moose looked interested but didn't say anything. It seemed a fitting end to an absolutely incredible trip. A lifelong memory for me, and I thought I was just having fun.

"What Ah You Lookin' Faw?"

Shortly after I graduated college, I was very fortunate to get a job at Connell & Associates. It was an engineering consulting firm in Coral Gables. I was hired to work in their newly-formed environmental department. There were four of us: the Vice President of the environmental department, a director, another ecologist fresh out of college, and me. This was indeed the beginning of an excellent opportunity for me – to be able to work in my field of Ecology, and the environmental work turned out to be a great opportunity for the company as well. The environmental department grew steadily during my time with the company.

The work was very exciting and rewarding. Some of our work was collecting data and information that would result in an Environmental Impact Statement (EIS), a Development of Regional Impact (DRI) statement, or more local environmental reports. Knowing that we were helping to protect the world around us and, almost daily, learning new things about the environment and the ecology of the area we were studying was a bonus.

We were also involved in many special studies, such as flora and fauna surveys and endangered species studies; these were my favorite projects. Every field trip was a new opportunity to learn more about the plants or animals we studied and their interaction with their environment. In the case of endangered species, the work entailed gathering information on the population size and working to understand why they became endangered and what could be done to help them flourish. Hopefully, to the point that they were no longer endangered and their population would sustain and grow.

As much as I enjoyed the fieldwork, there was a fair amount of time needed in the office to compile our data, analyze it, and of course, write the reports or papers. This was exciting as well. Sometimes, the information gathered in the field once studied and analyzed in the office would provide a different conclusion than I originally thought when I was in the field.

I have many stories to share about my work as an ecologist. But today's story is really about one time when I was in the office. The company had just gone through a major change. Another company bought it. The process was somewhat convoluted, but when all was said and done, the new company was Connel Metcalf & Eddy. That is another story in itself. As part of the company changes, we became more organized and efficient, and some new people were brought on board. One area where these changes took place was the supply room. A new person came on board to manage the supplies. He was very knowledgeable and helpful. He was from Boston and had a thick Bostonian accent. We became good friends.

On this particular day, I was in the office, writing a report, and needed something from the supply room. I was looking for whatever it was at the time when Frank walked in and asked me, "What ah you lookin' faw?" Without thinking, I said, "Peace of mind, Frank. Peace of mind." He just laughed and said, "I can't help you, theyah," and walked out of the room.

The thing is, I didn't know that I was going to say that until the words came out of my mouth. And, the thing is, I meant it.

We are all looking for peace of mind whenever we can find it. That's a good thing. I think that actively and deliberately being part of nature often helps to bring us peace of mind.

"The best remedy for those who are afraid, lonely, or unhappy is to go outside, somewhere where they can be quite alone with the heavens, nature and God. Because only then does one feel that all is as it should be and that God wishes to see people happy amidst the simple beauty of nature. ...I firmly believe that nature brings solace in all troubles."

— *Anne Frank*

PASSAGE 7

Owen Gromme

For a few years in the late '70s through the mid-'80s, I started and operated a mail-order bookshop named *The Naturalist Bookshop*. In 1984, I attended the American Booksellers Association's annual convention in Washington, DC. It was a brand new experience for me, though I had been in the book-selling business for several years. I started the bookshop with zero experience selling books or selling anything through the mail. My main goal was to make books on the Natural Sciences available to as many people as possible. To share my love of science and nature.

I learned many things by figuring out what and how to do things with the bookshop that have helped me throughout my life. But, as I said, those stories are for another time. Right now, I want to talk about Owen Gromme. A renowned and my absolute favorite wildlife artist. He was referred to as the "Dean of American Wildlife Artists" during his lifetime. He was also a devout environmentalist. At a commencement address in 1978, Gromme pointed out, "We owe a great deal to those who came before us, and it is our duty to pass on to prosper a world morally and physically, as good or better than the one we live in. It is our duty to oppose those who, out of greed and avarice, or for selfish or other reasons, would pollute, defile, or destroy that which means life itself to every living being."

So when I came upon the Stanton & Lee Publishers booth at the convention and looked through their featured work: *The World of Owen Gromme*, I was blown away. What a masterpiece of wildlife illustrations! Well, I am proud to say that I sold several copies of Owen's book, and of course, I have my copy that I regularly look through with great enjoyment. My favorite illustration is that of the "Virginia Deer with Fawns."

Photo credit: Leigh Yawkey Woodsen Art Museum

Owen wrote:

"One day, I very carefully observed this doe and her two fawns as they approached the water for a drink. The sun shone behind the animals, causing the light to filter delicately through their ears, making the ears seem almost translucent. The mother is a scrawny doe, with her ribs and loins showing; most does are quite lean this time of year since the nursing fawns keep their mother's weight down and she has a few scars on her skin where she has been tangled in barbed wire fences. But she makes a beautiful picture with her new fawns."

Each illustration is accompanied by Owen's story of how that painting came to be. The illustrations show the wildlife in an active state.

So, if you feel inclined, get your copy of *The World of Owen Gromme*, or check out some of his illustrations online. While you enjoy his beautiful art, remember what he wants us all to do: To protect and preserve our wondrous planet for "every living being."

Orange Tailed Squirrels

We live where there are a lot of oak trees, live oaks, and laurel oaks mostly. Some beautiful old trees with lots of Spanish moss hanging down. It's a squirrel's paradise. I've estimated the age of some of the live oak trees to be more than 300 years old, as I said, a squirrel's paradise.

We have three species of squirrels that live in our area:

1.) The southern flying squirrel. It's a small squirrel found in the treetops. Usually around 8 to 10 inches long. They can glide around 30 to 50 feet from tree to tree. It is pretty cool when you think about it.

2.) The Fox squirrel is fairly large with a long foxlike tail. This squirrel can grow to over 2 feet long. It varies in coloration but can be reddish-brown with a black head and white ears. Very distinctive and very pretty.

3.) Then there is the Eastern Gray Squirrel. It's a medium-size squirrel that is found throughout the Eastern United States. Usually, it is gray with some brownish color tones on its head and sides. I say usually because, in the past spring, we had two of our gray squirrels who turned up with orange tails. Bright orange tails. Apparently, this happens sometimes with gray squirrels.

Let me digress for just a little bit now. The squirrels in our yard and I get along very well. We have reached an arrangement over the years. I have a couple of bird feeders in the yard, and over the years, I have tried various configurations and methods to use the bird feeders just to feed the birds. From the very beginning, the squirrels have had different thoughts about this. They feel the birdseed is for them.

I've tried different types of bird feeders specifically designed to keep squirrels out. To no avail, I have used different methods of hanging the feeders. Again, to no avail. I've tried different areas of the yard. There was no difference. I have even tried talking to them with no effect. They look interested, but I don't think they're listening.

So, I've come to accept that when it comes to finding a way to get to the birds' food, the squirrels are smarter than me. As a result, I've put out a feeder just for the squirrels. They still get in the bird feeders from time to time but not nearly as often.

Back to the orange-tailed squirrels, they don't behave any different than the gray-tailed gray squirrels. They also don't behave any differently towards the gray-tailed squirrels, and the gray-tailed gray squirrels don't behave any differently towards them. They chase one another from time to time across the yard or round and round a tree. In general, they seem to be having fun together as only squirrels can.

Just a Bird

A couple of years ago, I was working in my backyard. I was standing on the corner of the bricked area next to our Koi pond trimming some plants we have in pots when a bird flew down and landed at my feet. It was a ring-necked dove. The beautiful bird began walking around a couple of feet from my feet. It definitely landed there deliberately and seemed to want something.

So I struck up a conversation.

I talk to animals and plants all the time. Like my morning songs I have written about earlier, I thought everybody does this. However, I understand now that most people don't. And like my morning songs, I've done it for as long as I can remember. I enjoy it. I think they do as well. See what you think after you have read my story.

So, after some casual conversation with the dove-like, "Hi. How's it going? And what have you been up to?" I asked it (I don't know if it was a male or female dove). "Are you hungry? Would you like something to eat?" I decided the answer was yes, and told it that I would get some birdseed and be right back. I thought as I started to walk away, it would fly away, but it didn't. So I went to the garage, got a handful of birdseed, and walked back to the dove. I had fully expected it to be gone at this point, but it wasn't. So, I put the seed on the ground next to it, and it started to eat. While it enjoyed the breakfast I brought, I continued to carry on with our conversation; granted, somewhat one-sided. The bird was really hungry, and the food was gone after a while. So, naturally, I told it I would get some more. Again, when I came back, the dove was still there and began eating the seed I put next to it. After a little more conversation, it flew up to a nearby tree branch and looked down at me for a little while. I took it as its way of saying thank you and it flew off.

I was very touched by this encounter...

A couple of weeks later, a similar thing happened to me. This time, it was a Robin. I was walking up the brick steps to our Koi pond when I saw a Robin sitting on the wooden fence a few feet away. So, of course, I struck up a conversation, "Hey. How's it going? Why are you still here? Your buddies flew up North a couple of weeks ago." And then, of course, I asked if it were hungry, "Would it like some worms?" Deciding that it was a yes, I went to dig up some worms in the yard, expecting that when I got back to the bird, it would be gone. It wasn't. So, I set the worms down on the brick steps and stood back a few feet. The Robin flew down and ate the worms. I did this several more times over the next couple of days, and then it was gone. Hopefully, it was able to meet up with its flock up North.

I think you will have to admit these were two fairly remarkable interactions with wildlife. I have always felt a connection to Mother Earth and our fellow inhabitants, plants, and animals. I feel very strongly that we are all in this together, that we need to look out for one another, that as human beings, we have a responsibility to do all we can to help preserve and protect our Mother Earth.

"Preserve and cherish the pale blue dot, the only home we've ever known."

— *Carl Sagan*

We All Need Our Own Space

Blue whales are the largest animal on the planet. They can grow to over 100 feet long and weigh up to 130 tons (260,000 pounds). At birth, a blue whale calf is around 23 feet long and will weigh 5,000 to 6,000 pounds. They need a lot of space. On the other hand, an adult sea otter grows to 4 or 5 feet and weighs around 100 pounds. When the mothers dive for food, they tie their babies into kelp to ensure that they will not float away (just a fun observation).

The thing is, they share the same ocean. However, they require a very different space within the ocean – just by virtue of who they are.

The same is true for plants as well. A redwood tree can grow up to be 300 feet tall and more than 20 feet in diameter. Just as an aside, they capture more carbon dioxide than any other tree on earth. They need a lot of space.

Sea Oats, on the other hand, grow up to around 6 feet tall at maturity and have leaves around 2 feet long. It tolerates salt spray, grows near the ocean shore, and is vital in shoreline stabilization.

Zooplankton (tiny animals) and phytoplankton (tiny plants) range in size from 2 micrometers (smaller than a human red blood cell) up to several inches. They drift in large bodies of water, such as the oceans and lakes. An individual plankton doesn't take up much space but as small as they are, they are immensely important to life on earth.

People take up space too. Human beings need their own space, just like every other plant and animal on our planet.

The point is, we all take up space, and we all should give each other their own space.

Volume is the three-dimensional space occupied by a substance or enclosed by a surface. The formula for determining the volume of space an object takes up is: $l \times w \times h$; where 'l' is **length**, 'w' is **width**, and 'h' is **height**.

Personal space for humans is the distance from another person at which one feels comfortable when talking to or being next to that other person.

Well, to some extent, plants and animals need their personal space as well. Have you ever been dive-bombed by a mockingbird, for instance, because it felt you were getting too close to its nest? Or, did you ever wonder why trees in the wild need so much space between them and their neighbors to grow properly?

A honey bee hive may hold 2000 bees and have a volume of only around two cubic feet. However, the bees need approximately an acre (43,560 square feet) of wild blossoming flowers, trees, and shrubs to survive.

Human beings need space in a similar way that honey bees do. We live in homes that take up a relatively smaller area than what we need to survive. Many of us go to the supermarket to get the food we need, but that food is grown, cultivated, and raised over large areas.

So, to be healthy, to grow, and to get along together in this great big beautiful world, we all need our own space.

A Picture is Worth a Thousand Words

A beautiful sunrise presents so many possibilities. Technically, sunrise is the time in the morning when the sun first appears. But it's so much more than that. It's the start of a new day on that part of the planet where we live and sets in motion a myriad of events that define our day.

I'll Tell You How the Sun Rose by Emily Dickinson

I'll tell you how the Sun rose –
A Ribbon at a time –
The Steeples swam in Amethyst –
The news, like Squirrels, ran –
The Hills untied their Bonnets –
The Bobolinks – begun –
Then I said softly to myself –
"That must have been the Sun"

So, it's not just people that are waking up with the sun. The entire earth awakens when the first rays of morning light fall upon it. And, of course, it's not just the light but also the warmth that sets everything in motion. Mother Earth has played this tune for eons, and every piece of the planet plays its part. As the first rays of light fall upon the oceans, lakes, and streams, the microscopic zooplankton start their daily migration downward in the water column, only to rise again at sunset. Birds awaken and, along with countless other animals, start their daily search for food.

"The early bird gets the worm."

Most animals are diurnal – awake and active during the day. Some animals are nocturnal – awake and active at night. These animals go to sleep when the sun rises or before.

Many plants begin the process of photosynthesis at sunrise, turning sunlight, carbon dioxide (that humans, for instance, exhale with every breath), and water into food, releasing oxygen in the process. In this process, plants transfer energy from the sun to make sugar (food), to be used or stored later, which is not a bad deal for us humans and other oxygen-breathing organisms on the planet. And then there is all the food that the plants make that we humans and other animals depend on to survive—quite a remarkable reciprocal relationship between the plants and animals on our planet.

Of course, the light from the first rays of the sun allows us to see just what's going on around us, including the sunrise. We depend on this light to see and interact with the world, or we create artificial light sources so we can see well at night. Cats, however, don't need artificial light at night. They have 6 to 8 times more rod cells in their eyes than we do. These rods are the cells most sensitive to low light giving cats the night vision advantage over us. However, cats don't perceive all the colors we do and many other animals see colors that we can't.

With the sunrise, the earth itself starts to warm and expand, causing to some extent the crumbling of mountains to the sea. The sun warms the soil and rocks and boulders that might be used by certain cold-blooded animals, such as lizards, even very big lizards such as Komodo Dragons, to warm themselves. It allows the Anhinga (a black long-necked fish-eating bird that "swims" underwater and spears fish with their long pointed bills) to dry its wings after breakfast. Anhinga don't have very good oil glands, so they are able to dive deep underwater to chase fish. But because of this, it must dry its wings before it can fly.

The warmth from the sun will cause the snow to melt on a Colorado mountain top and flow, in a sparkling clear stream, to the river in the valley below and ultimately to the sea.

The morning sun heats the air as well, and as it heats up, it rises, and a breeze stirs, a breeze that cools us on a hot summer day. This upward flow of heated air carries with it, among other things, moisture. On a summer's day, this water vapor and dust might turn into cumulonimbus clouds that later may rain or even form a thunderstorm with lightning and thunder and perhaps a rainbow at the end.

The sun gives us energy as well. The light we see as the sun peeks over the horizon in the morning is literally a transference of energy from our star to us and everything on our planet.

The sunrise provides a brand new canvas for us every day and an opportunity to fill our minds and hearts with the beauty and wonder that surrounds us. That gives us hope and anticipation of good things to come. How can one look at a sunrise and not sense this?

A sunrise can be simply inspirational.

Morning Has Broken - Eleanor Farjeon

Morning has broken like the first morning
Blackbird has spoken like the first bird
Praise for the singing
Praise for the morning
Praise for them springing fresh from the Word
Sweet the rain's new fall, sunlit from heaven
Like the first dew fall on the first grass
Praise for the sweetness of the wet garden
Sprung in completeness where His feet pass
Mine is the sunlight
Mine is the morning
Born of the One Light Eden saw play
Praise with elation, praise every morning
God's recreation of the new day
Morning has broken like the first morning
Blackbird has spoken like the first bird
Praise for the singing
Praise for the morning
Praise for them springing fresh from the Word
https://www.youtube.com/watch?v=we-n-Zmglt0

So, at the end of this entry, I have written one thousand words about the photo of a sunrise taken some years back. I could write many thousands more. Do you have a photo or a picture that inspires you to write a thousand words about it?

Why not write about a picture you think is worth a thousand words or even more. It can be very relaxing and sometimes revealing. There is a reason that:

"A Picture is Worth a Thousand Words"

The Bonnie Banks of Loch Lomond

I remember, as a child, my father would often sing songs in the house or while my brothers and sisters and I were riding in the car with him. He had a remarkable baritone voice. When he was a young man, he sang in the chorus at times in the Metropolitan Opera in New York City. He sang many different songs during our childhood, but there is one in particular that has always been dear to my heart: "The Bonnie Banks of Loch Lomond." As time has gone by, I have carried on my father's tradition, and I sing songs to myself and my family and to anyone who will listen from time to time, including "The Bonnie Banks of Loch Lomond."

I have always loved this somewhat melancholy tune, and even though the story is very sad, it's still a beautiful song. Little did I know how sad the story behind the music was until recently. I thought it was about two young lovers that had a falling out. I never really understood what was meant by the *high road* and the *low road* and why they would never meet again, and I'm half Scots on my mother's side – a Malcolm.

Here is a particularly beautiful rendition of this haunting Scottish song:

https://www.youtube.com/watch?v=gb8AGuD2uOI

A few days ago, my morning song (I always wake up with a morning song) was "The Bonnie Banks of Loch Lomond." I keep an ongoing list of my morning songs now, and in the process of finding this particularly beautiful version by Ella Roberts above, I thought I would look up who wrote the song and maybe a little bit of its history. I was not prepared for what I found:

"The Bonnie Banks of Loch Lomond"

The words *were written by Andrew Lang around 1876*

Historical Background: From Frank Ticheli - Manhattan Beach Music

The song is based on the traditional belief that your soul will return to your home before you go to heaven, so beautiful.

At the time in Scottish history when "Loch Lomond" was a new song, the United Kingdom (which is: United Scotland, England, and Wales) had already been formed. But the Highland Scots wanted a Scottish, not an English, King to rule. Led by their Bonnie Prince Charlie (Prince Charles Edward Stuart), they attempted unsuccessfully to depose Britain's, King George II. An army of 7,000 Highlanders was defeated on April 16, 1746, at the famous Battle of Culloden Moor.

It is this same battle that indirectly gives rise to this beautiful song. After the battle, many Scottish soldiers were imprisoned within England's Carlisle Castle, near the border of Scotland. "Loch Lomond," tells the story of two Scottish soldiers who were so imprisoned. One of them was to be executed, while the other was to be set free. According to Celtic legend, if someone dies in a foreign land, his spirit will travel to his homeland by "the low road" - the route for the souls of the dead. In the song, the spirit of the dead soldier shall arrive first, while the living soldier will take the "high road" over the mountains to arrive afterward.

The song is from the point of view of the soldier who will be executed: When he sings, "ye'll tak' the high road and I'll tak' the low road," in effect, he is saying that you will return alive, and I will return in spirit. He remembers his happy past, "By yon bonnie banks ... where me and my true love were ever wont to gae [accustomed to go]" and sadly accepts his death "the broken heart it ken nae [knows no] second Spring again."

The song takes on a whole new meaning for me now. Of course, it still has a beautiful and engaging melody. But knowing the story and the history behind the words now makes it, to me, even sadder. Throughout mankind's history, I wonder how many poems have been written? How many songs have been sung about the fallout of war? Our written history, since the very beginning, has been filled with the horrors that we have inflicted on ourselves through our wars. How many times has someone taken the low road to never meet their true love again? How do we make it stop? Something very much worth putting some thought into and striving for, I think. Not just living in peace and harmony with one another but with all our fellow "earth-born companions" and our magnificent planet Mother Earth.

PASSAGE 9

Crescendo

I wrote this piece some time back. I suppose, today, some of the items would be referred to as my bucket list. It was written long before the term was coined. Some of the items are transcendental, intentionally so. Some of the items fall in the "it doesn't hurt to want" category. This is a saying my wife has used with me from time to time. It was passed on to her from her Grandfather. It can be very profound at times. Some items are for others to decide if I have accomplished them already or if I am in the process of accomplishing them or not. I certainly hope that I am and that I have. Other things are still out there to be done, along with many new things to add to the list. Hopefully, life is dynamic and full of good surprises. Isn't that a wonderful thing?

A friend asked me the other day, "Well, what would you like to do?" I don't think she was prepared for my answer.

I would like to: perform surgery that saves someone's life, hunt for dinosaur bones in Montana, explore the Galapagos Islands and water ski on Lake Michigan, I want to see the Parthenon and touch Stonehenge, I want to go horseback riding where King Arthur did, and practice sorcery as Merlin did.

I want to see the world through a child's eyes again. I want to make people laugh. I want to write a poem that has a different meaning every time you read it. I want to be a good Dad. I want the world to be a better place because I was in it. I want to love a woman so much it hurts, and I want her to love me right back. I want to see a meteor shower and a sun shower. I want to shower the people I love with warmth and kindness. I want to be a good person. I want to help.

I want to catch a hundred-pound Tarpon and let it go. I want to fly like the wind and grow flowers. I want to get up early and stay up late. I want to be smart. I want to live life to the fullest, with each day a new and exciting adventure.

Wiglaf – Hope of the Future

Sometime back, I wrote about a poem I first read in my 11th grade English Literature class, "To a Mouse" by Robert Burns. This class opened up a whole new world for me. The teacher was so knowledgeable and passionate about English Literature. She brought poetry and prose to life. She made many trips to England to visit the places where the romantic poets and others lived and where they wrote their stories or poetry. She brought this passion and love for English Literature to every class. She was one of those people in my life that opened a door for me. I will share many more stories with you about my time in one of my favorite classes, but this time, I want to share my thoughts on a particular heroic poem we studied: Beowulf.

The thing that struck me about Beowulf from the first time I read it was the role Wiglaf played in the epic tale. Of course, Beowulf is the hero. The fearless warrior saves the day not once but twice by slaying the monsters Grendel and then Grendel's mother. After these heroic deeds, Beowulf becomes king and rules for fifty peaceful years. And so the tale could end here with Beowulf, a true hero and a great leader. But, just as with mankind, there is more to the story. There is a continuum. As Sonny and Cher would say, "The Beat Goes On."

https://www.youtube.com/watch?v=u6l2jnazVFM.

As I read the part at the end of this remarkable tale, I had a picture in my mind's eye of Beowulf giving his all once again to slay the dragon but slowly failing and Wiglaf running up the hill to help his master, his mentor, with the sunlight shining down through the dark clouds on him, Wiglaf – the hope of the future. I have always wished I could recreate this scene on canvas. To capture the solemn yet triumphant feeling of mankind passing the torch, so to speak, to the younger generations, the new saviors of our grand journey, the hope of the future.

Alas, I'm no artist. I do well with three-dimensional sculpture-type work but just can't seem to get the proper perspectives onto the surface of a page. Perhaps, someone out there would like to capture this moment on paper.

Wiglaf running up the hill to help his master, his mentor, with the sunlight shining down through the dark clouds on him.

Some Old Poetry

I came across a folder of some poetry I wrote many years ago. The poems seem to be as compelling today as they were years ago, to me anyway. I hope you find them of some interest, and perhaps they will cause you to pause and take some "time to think" for just a bit.

Lost Youth

Once long ago, so very long ago

There was a certain kind of magic in life

That let you see suffering,

Without suffering yourself

That let you hurt

Without feeling the pain

That let you view death

But left you feeling indestructible

That let you be at peace

When all around you was in turmoil

Oh how I wish for those days gone by,

When I could laugh, when I could cry

When everything was so important,

But never really mattered

Freedom

Freedom comes with early Spring
Your colors really show then
Expressed to their fullest
Unburdened by Summer's heat and conformity
Not shackled by Autumn's cold winds
Or the heavy snows of Winter

Time

Time to breath, time to think
Time to laugh...and cry
Time to live with the Earth
And reach for the sky
Time to slow down so the
World won't pass me by

Happy Tune

The leaves are blowing in the breeze
The sun is shining down on me
The birds are singing in the trees
I'm as happy as can be

Passage 10

To Us All

To a Mouse - On Turning Her Up in Her Nest With the Plough, November 1785, is a poem by Robert Burns.

"To a Mouse"

(Translated into Modern English)

Small, crafty, cowering, timorous little beast,

O, what a panic is in your little breast!

You need not start away so hasty

With argumentative chatter!

I would be loath to run and chase you,

With murdering plough-staff.

I'm truly sorry man's dominion

Has broken Nature's social union,

And justifies that ill opinion

Which makes you startle at me,

your poor, earth-born companion

And fellow mortal!

I doubt not, sometimes, but you may steal;

What then? Poor little beast, you must live!

An odd ear in twenty-four sheaves

Is a small request;
I will get a blessing with what is left,
And never miss it.

Your small house, too, in ruin!
Its feeble walls the winds are scattering!
And nothing now, to build a new one,
Of coarse grass green!
And bleak December's winds coming,
Both bitter and keen!

You saw the fields laid bare and wasted,
And weary winter coming fast,
And cozy here, beneath the blast,
You thought to dwell,
Till crash! The cruel plough passed
Out through your cell.

That small bit heap of leaves and stubble,
Has cost you many a weary nibble!
Now you are turned out, for all your trouble,
Without house or holding,
To endure the winter's sleety dribble,
And hoar-frost cold.

But little Mouse, you are not alone,
In proving foresight may be vain:
The best-laid schemes of mice and men
Go often awry,
And leave us nothing but grief and pain,

For promised joy!

Still you are blessed, compared with me!

The present only touches you:

But oh! I backward cast my eye,

On prospects dreary!

And forward, though I cannot see,

I guess and fear!

I'm half Scottish, a Malcolm on my mother's side. I'm also a Naturalist/Ecologist and a great admirer of poetry, the romantic poets, and the romantic period in England. Burns was a pre-romantic poet and is the national poet of Scotland. I think it's important to remember the period in history when he wrote his poetry.

It was during my 11th grade English Literature class that I first read "To a Mouse" by Robert Burns. The poem made quite an impact on me on many levels. I could just feel the pain it caused Burns upon discovering he had ruined this poor mouse's nest. Also, he felt that he and the mouse were both on the same level as "earth-born companions." I feel the same way about our fellow inhabitants on our planet. We are all in this together. Then there is the line, "The best-laid schemes of mice and men go often awry," The depth of feeling and understanding of human nature in this one line is overpowering.

There is so much more to explore about this poem. I think, for now, placing all living creatures on the planet on the same level as far as sharing the planet and all of us, plants and animals, trying every day to make a living and survive is enough.

One more thing about Robert Burns is that he wrote "Auld Lang Syne" in 1788.

I will say this, for someone who was, for a period in his life, a poor tenant farmer. Someone who did not have the comforts that many of us enjoy today. Robert Burns, for centuries now, has inspired mankind to appreciate that we are all part of nature, to reflect on our lives, and be the best we can be so we don't go awry too often. And to honor our feelings of nostalgia and love of old relationships from times gone by.

"To a Mouse"

(As Burns wrote it in Scottish Dialect)

Wee, sleeket, cowran, tim'rous beastie,

O, what a panic's in thy breastie!

Thou need na start awa sae hasty,

Wi' bickerin brattle!

I wad be laith to rin an' chase thee

Wi' murd'ring pattle!

I'm truly sorry Man's dominion

Has broken Nature's social union,

An' justifies that ill opinion,

Which makes thee startle,

At me, thy poor, earth-born companion,

An' fellow-mortal!

I doubt na, whyles, but thou may thieve;

What then? poor beastie, thou maun live!

A daimen-icker in a thrave

'S a sma' request:

I'll get a blessin wi' the lave,

An' never miss 't!

Thy wee-bit housie, too, in ruin!

It's silly wa's the win's are strewin!

An' naething, now, to big a new ane,

O' foggage green!

An' bleak December's winds ensuin,

Baith snell an' keen!

Thou saw the fields laid bare an' waste,

An' weary Winter comin fast,
An' cozie here, beneath the blast,
Thou thought to dwell,
Till crash! the cruel coulter past
Out thro' thy cell.
That wee-bit heap o' leaves an' stibble
Has cost thee monie a weary nibble!
Now thou's turn'd out, for a' thy trouble,
But house or hald,
To thole the Winter's sleety dribble,
An' cranreuch cauld!
But Mousie, thou art no thy-lane,
In proving foresight may be vain:
The best laid schemes o' Mice an' Men
Gang aft agley,
An' lea'e us nought but grief an' pain,
For promis'd joy!
Still, thou art blest, compar'd wi' me!
The present only toucheth thee:
But Och! I backward cast my e'e,
On prospects drear!
An' forward tho' I canna see,
I guess an' fear!

Serpentine Sunday

I recently unearthed a short story I started writing many years ago when I was in college at the University of Miami. I grew up in South Miami along with four brothers and two sisters. There were ten of us altogether, including my mother and father and my grandmother on my mother's side. I was number six out of seven children.

My parents both worked, so my brothers and I had plenty of free time after school. One of our favorite things was to catch snakes in the abandoned tomato fields near our house. We made an arrangement with Dr. Haast of the Miami Serpentarium. He would give us a dime for each non-poisonous snake we brought in. So we spent our afternoons catching snakes, and almost every Saturday morning, we would take them out of the cages we had made for them in our backyard, put them in an old pillowcase and take them to Dr. Haast. Many times, we had ten or twenty snakes in our sack.

My poor mother was terrified of snakes, and I know she worried that we would get hurt or bitten by a poisonous snake when we were out in the fields, but she allowed us to set up our snake cages in the backyard and drove us, snakes in a bag in the back seat to collect our bounty. She was in cahoots with us, part of the gang. I've often wondered why she would let us pursue such a dangerous venture. I think it's because she loved us so much. She was willing to set aside her fears because she knew how much we enjoyed it. She went to work every day, and I know she would much rather have stayed at home and spent time with her kids. Looking back on it now, I realize my mother trusted us. I think this trust made us feel responsible as kids and helped us grow up to be responsible adults.

My brother Pete was by far the best snake catcher. He was fast as lightning and fearless. For every snake I would catch, Pete would catch ten, but when we split up the money on Saturday, Pete made sure we split it evenly. Pete was just a year and four months older than me. Many people thought we were twins.

As we grew older, our interests changed. There were sports and girls in high school. As it turns out, Pete was as fast as lightning. He held the state record for the 220-yard dash for a while. I could never come close to Pete's speed, but I could run for a long time.

Later in college, I would take up long-distance running, something I have enjoyed my entire adult life. Isn't it funny how two children in the same family, so close together, can be so different?

While we were in college, Pete got married. He and his wife lived on Quail Roost Drive near where we grew up. It was a winding up and down the road, so much so that even if you drove slow, it felt like you were on a roller coaster. By the time you got to the main road, your stomach felt as if it was in your throat. When we were young, my brothers and I would be in the car with my mother driving down that road singing "Onward Christian Soldiers," one of her favorite songs. Now that I look back on it, Quail Roost Drive was my favorite road as a child growing up.

One summer afternoon, there was a ruckus in Pete's front yard. Cars had stopped on the side of the road, and people from these cars and some of his neighbors were throwing rocks at something. It was a twelve-foot Python. Pete got them to stop throwing rocks and, of course, caught the Python. The police came and took the snake to the Miami Serpentarium. The next day, Pete got a call from Dr. Haast. Would they like to come and see their snake and be their guest for the day? The answer was, "Yes, of course!"

Pete called and asked if I would like to join them. So the three of us went to spend Sunday afternoon at the Serpentarium. It would be like the good ole days.

We went to look at Pete's snake first. It was in a large cage that had a glass front. There was another Python in the cage about the same size. For a while, we had trouble figuring out which Python was Pete's, but eventually, we did, to our satisfaction anyway. It was a very large snake.

We walked around the Serpentarium for a while. The sun shone brightly, and it was so hot the air was hazy. We spent some time watching young alligators in their pit chasing turtles in the water. This one gator would try to bite the turtles, but every time he did, the slippery thing would squirt out of his mouth, just like someone spitting watermelon seeds. Though the alligator didn't tire of this, we finally did.

We went to the pit that held the really large alligators and crocodiles. Years before, we had brought Dr. Haast a speckled caiman we caught while fishing off Old Cutler Road. We wondered if he was in the pit, but that's a different story.

Dr. Haast was getting ready to "milk" some poisonous snakes, risking his life once again for the research he did and for the anti-venom that has saved so many lives around the world. We were going to watch but decided we had seen enough. Much of the magic of our childhood snake-catching days was gone.

I guess I liked tramping through the fields so much as a boy I decided to become a biologist, an ecologist, actually. Pete became a psychologist. He worked with troubled children. He was always giving so much of himself to bring happiness to others, just as my mother did. Pete died very young. He left behind a wife and three young children.

I think about Pete often and how life is sometimes like a serpentine journey. A little bit like my favorite road, it sometimes leaves you with your heart in your throat.

Life's Journey (Unfinished)

I saw the Loch Ness Monster
Sitting in a tree
I said, "Hello", as I walked by
She said hello to me
Down the road aways
The Purple People Eater stood
I decided to leave the path
And headed through the wood
I slipped on an orange banana peel
And fell onto a rocky shore
A crimson tide swept over me
And I was blue no more
The golden yellow sun appeared
And set my heart on fire
It burned so bright but emitted no light
You could hardly tell it was there
I doused it with the deep dark void
Of a lonely afternoon
Then all turned black; save for the twinkling stars
Till the sun replaced the moon
And with the dawn, the rain did come
The water rose to my throat
I decided to leave this place
And went looking for a boat
I sailed away to a distant land
That was desolate and bare
The only things that I could see

Were atom bombs falling through the air
I could not stay, I ran away
As fast as I could fly
A cloud passed by and asked me why
"Why not," was my reply
Then the lightning shattered the sky
It fell onto the ground
A million pieces of white and blue
And I was out of glue
And when the sun shone through
Everything turned hot and red
I escaped through a dark and narrow tunnel
I knew not where it led
I ran into a contradiction
He tried to drag me down
He said, "yes or no," I said I don't know
And everything began spinning around
The ground did tremble and shake
The walls came down on me
I thought my life was over
When forgiveness set me free
I found myself at the edge of a road
Standing next to a teddy bear
I asked the bear, "Where does this road lead?"
He just said, "Try it and see"
There's just one way to find out,
To get rid of your doubt,
And that's to try it and see,
And see,
And that's to try it and see"

www.ingramcontent.com/pod-product-compliance
Lightning Source LLC
Chambersburg PA
CBHW052025030426
42335CB00026B/3282